Art and Life in Rural Japan
Toho Village Through the Eyes of Its Youth

田園地域の工芸と暮らし
子供達の視点から見た東峰村

NEXT GENERATION PRESS

Edited by Cyrus Rolbin

Printed in Hong Kong by Great Wall Printing, Ltd.
Distributed by Next Generation Press

ISBN: 978-0-9815595-3-7
CIP data available.

Design assistance by Sandra Delany.

Next Generation Press, a not-for-profit book publisher, brings forward the
voices and vision of adolescents on their own lives, learning, and work.
With a particular focus on youth without economic privilege, Next Generation
Press raises awareness of young people as a powerful force for social justice.

Next Generation Press, P.O. Box 603252, Providence, Rhode Island 02906 U.S.A.
www.nextgenerationpress.org

10 9 8 7 6 5 4 3 2 1

Contents 目次

Foreword 前書き

BACK IN THE EARLY 1990s, when I was teaching English at a high school in southern Japan, one of my students and his father once took me on a day trip to Koishiwara, a remote mountain village renowned for its traditional stoneware. The pottery was stunning and I ended up buying much more of it than I could afford; but that first trip to Koishiwara inspired more than just my hidden shopper. With its pristine air and water, lush scenery, natural local foods, and graceful, artistic spirit, Koishiwara embodied the idyllic charm of old Japan that had lured me to that country, but which has all but disappeared from its urban areas.

Nearly two decades later, when I was teaching at Keio University over 500 miles away, I was taken aback by a colleague's invitation to join a revitalization project in a village in southern Japan "formerly known as Koishiwara." Since the 1980s, the populations of Koishiwara and neighboring Hoshuyama had steadily shrunk, like those of most small municipalities throughout the country, and in 2005 the two villages had been forced to merge into a new one that they named Toho. Even after the merger, however, Toho's population had continued to decrease, and in 2007 the governor of Fukuoka Prefecture had called upon Keio University for help. I had never imagined that my work might lead me back to that nostalgic place.

The revitalization effort mainly focused on supporting the village's plan to promote itself through media production and use of the Internet – a particular challenge, as Toho had the dubious distinction of being the last community in southern Japan to obtain broadband access. At Keio I had been running a seminar on youth-based educational media production, and so I decided to try working with some of Toho's younger residents on films that introduced the village from their points of view.

During the summer of 2007, five of my students and I stayed in Toho and ran a video production camp for nine children – nearly ten percent of the population under the age of fifteen. The children produced films that introduced Koishiwara ware and other village products in a gameshow-style format.

In October of that year, my students and I presented our project at Harvard Graduate School of Education. Later, a reporter who covered that event introduced me to Barbara Cervone,

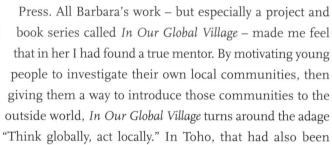

president of the nonprofit organization What Kids Can Do, Inc. (WKCD; www.whatkidscando.org) and its book publishing arm, Next Generation Press. All Barbara's work – but especially a project and book series called *In Our Global Village* – made me feel that in her I had found a true mentor. By motivating young people to investigate their own local communities, then giving them a way to introduce those communities to the outside world, *In Our Global Village* turns around the adage "Think globally, act locally." In Toho, that had also been exactly our project's focus. Over the next several months, I started working with children in Toho again. This time, we would produce a book for the *In Our Global Village* series.

The Toho students first examined copies of books that other youth had created for the series: *In Our Village*, by children in the village of Kambi ya Simba in Tanzania (www.inourvillage.org); *India in a Time of Globalization*, by young people from three cities in India; and *West Hollywood Through the Eyes of Its Youth*, by students in Los Angeles, California. Then we discussed what the Toho children envisioned for their own book. They took their first round of photos in the fall of 2008, and that winter an elementary school teacher in upstate New York, a colleague of Barbara's, asked her students to comment on them. That feedback gave the children

a sense of how young people in the West perceived Japan in general, and which aspects of Toho seemed most interesting to them. Most important, the sheer evidence of interest in their village – and in their own presentation of it – by young people overseas inspired the Toho youth to put their hearts and minds into this project.

In the summer of 2009, a colleague of mine traveled to Toho to run a photography workshop, during which the children took over 1,200 new photos. The children sent their favorites to me along with written comments, and we started to put the book together.

As with other volumes in the *In Our Global Village* series, this book combines the diverse creativity and perspectives of several young photographer-authors. In order to achieve coherence without imposing my own voice on the text, I asked the children to participate in the editing process as well.

Our book presents the original Japanese sentences along with their English translations. We hope that this will make it possible for a wide range of readers – including English-language students in Japan and Japanese-language students throughout the world – to enjoy and learn from it. As for readers who have never studied Japanese, we hope that the visual presence of the Japanese text will make it easier for them to travel in their minds from wherever they may be to this precious, precarious village in the mountains of southern Japan.

Cyrus Rolbin
Chestnut Hill, Massachusetts
U.S.A.

A Tiny Village in a Country of Cities

As you can see from how brightly it shines from space at night, Japan is one of the most urbanized countries in the world.

都会の国の中の小さな村

Japan ▶

宇宙から見える夜の光り方から分かりますように、日本は世界で一番
都会的な国の一つです。

Population and Land Mass of Japan and USA, 2010
日本とアメリカの人口と面積（２０１０年）

	Population 人口	Land Mass (km² / mi²) 面積 (km² / mi²)
Japan	127,000,000	377,873 / 145,883
USA	300,000,000	9,826,675 / 3,794,101

Source: United Nations Population Database

Japan's population amounts to more than a third of the population in the United States, but its land mass is only 1/26th.

日本の人口はアメリカのほぼ３分の１ですが、面積は２６分の１です。

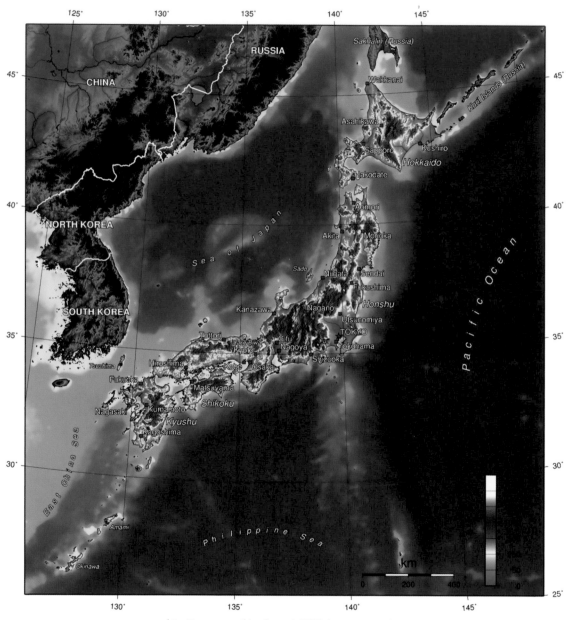

http://commons.wikimedia.org/wiki/File:Japan_topo_en.jpg

8

Over three-fourths of Japan is covered by mountains, so most of our country has a very high population density.

国の３／４以上が山地で占められているので、日本の人口密度はとても高いです。

Selected Countries by Population Density, 2010
各国の人口密度（２０１０年）

Country 国	World Rank 世界順位	Population Density (人口密度) km²	mi²
Macau	1	18,534	48,003
Singapore	3	7,022	18,189
Taiwan	16	639	1,656
South Korea	22	487	1,260
India	31	359	929
Japan	**36**	**337**	**873**
Philippines	43	307	796
United Kingdom	51	255	660
China	78	139	361
USA	178	32	83
New Zealand	200	16	41
Australia	233	2.9	7.5

Source: United Nations Population Database

This is the city of Fukuoka.

It has a population of over 1,450,000 people and is located just 45 km (28 mi) from our village.

これは福岡市です。

人口は１４５万人以上で、私達の村から
４５キロしか離れていません。

Fukuoka

This is Toho, our village.

これが私達の東峰村です。

Our way of life is not well known to most people who live in Japanese cities,
let alone the rest of the world.

私達の生活は日本の都会に住んでいる人々や、まして海外の人々などには、
ほとんど知られていません。

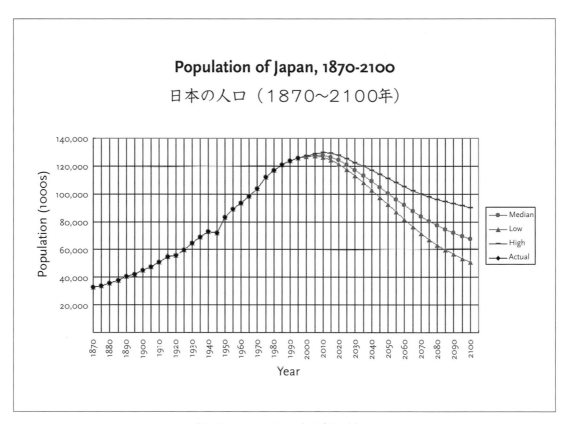

Population of Japan, 1870-2100

日本の人口（1870〜2100年）

It is also in jeopardy. A severe depopulation trend in Japan is expected to continue for several decades, and it is affecting villages much more than metropolitan areas.

そして不安定でもあります。と言うのも、日本ではこれから人口減少が数十年間続くと予想されていますが、その影響は都会より村の方がより深刻だからです。

Japan's birthrate has been decreasing for the past thirty-five years, and according to the Japanese government it is falling faster than that of any other country. In 2009, children under the age of fifteen made up only 13 percent of the population.

日本の出生率は３５年前から下がってきていて、日本政府の調べによると、どの国よりも早く減りつつあると言われています。２００９年時点で、１５才未満の子供が人口の１３％しかいません。

On top of the low birthrate, children living in rural areas are becoming more and more attracted to city life, and also anxious about the limited variety of jobs that are available where they live.

そのうえ、田舎に住んでいる子供達がしだいに都会の生活に惹かれたり、地元での仕事の選択が少ないことに不安を感じています。

Great Heisei-Era Mergers, 1999–2006
平成大合併（１９９９〜２００６年）

Municipality	市町村	1999	2006
Cities	市	670	779
Towns	町	1,994	844
Villages	村	568	197
Total	合計	3,232	1,820

Source: Japanese Ministry of Internal Affairs and Communications

Small towns and villages cannot receive enough tax money from residents to keep functioning, and so they depend heavily on the government. In the 1990s, the federal government decided it could not continue to give the same amount of support to those smaller communities, and so it changed the tax system to persuade neighboring ones to merge with each other. As a result, from 1999 to 2006 the number of villages in Japan decreased by 65 percent.

小さな町や村が機能するためには、住民からの税金だけでは補えず政府に大きく頼っています。９０年代に、政府が市町村への交付金を従来通りに維持できなくなり、そして隣接した市町村の合併を促すために地方交付税の制度を変えました。その結果、１９９９年〜２００６年の間で村の数が６５％ほど減りました。

hō shu yama

宝珠山

ko ishi wara

小石原

In the past, the village we now call Toho was made up of two separate villages: Hoshuyama and Koishiwara. Each had its own industries and local identity which had developed over hundreds of years.

現在「東峰村」と呼ばれている地域は、以前は「宝珠山」と「小石原」という個別の村でした。それぞれの村には数百年間で発達してきた独自の産業や地域の誇りがありました。

The two villages decided to merge in 2005. Even after their populations were combined, though, the newly formed village had only 2,749 residents, making it the smallest merged village in Japan.

2つの村は2005年に合併することにしました。両方の人口を合わせても2、749人で、全国で当時合併した村の中で一番人口が少ない村でした。

This is Toho's official logo. It symbolizes two mountain villages joining together in harmony.

これが東峰村のロゴマークです。山の中の２つの村が一緒に力を合わせて行くという意味が込められています。

In this book we will introduce some of Toho's history, industries, daily life, things to see and do, and the effects of depopulation from our point of view.

この本では、東峰村の歴史、産業、私達の日常生活、一番好きなことや
もの、そして過疎化の影響などについて紹介します。

Getting Around
交通手段

Clickety-clack...

That's the sound of the *Hita-hikosan sen,* the only train that passes through our village.

「ガタンゴトン…」

これが私達の村を通る、たった一つの日田彦山線という電車の走っている音です。

Because there is no direct route to Fukuoka (45 km [28 mi] away), it takes over two hours to get there using this train.

福岡市までは直行ルートがないので、２時間以上かかります。

Still, the image of the single yellow train car, especially when it passes over Toho's three "eyeglass bridges" is one of the most cherished symbols of our village.

Every year in late December, the bridges are illuminated at night.

それでも、その黄色い一車両の電車とその電車が通る「めがね橋」は村の人々に愛されているシンボルです。

毎年１２月後半の夜、めがね橋がライトアップされています。

Population Density, 2010
人口密度（２０１０年）

	km²	mi²
Japan	337	873
Toho Village	45	131

Sources: United Nations
Population Database and http://wapedia.mobi/ja/東峰村

Toho's population is spread out over 52 km² (20 mi²), about half of which is covered by mountains.

約半分が山地で占められている村の総面積５２km²の中に、村の人々が住んでいます。

On top of the limited train transportation, each day only six buses pass through the village. Especially since the merger, most kids have to depend on their parents to get around.

電車での交通の不便さに加えて、バスの本数も１日６本しかありません。特に合併後、村の子供達が、移動するためには親に頼らざるを得ません。

Art of the People

The mountains of Koishiwara are rich in clay deposits that villagers have used to make pottery for over 400 years.

民衆の芸術

小石原の山には、４００年以上、村の人々が焼物を作るために使って
いる土壌があります。

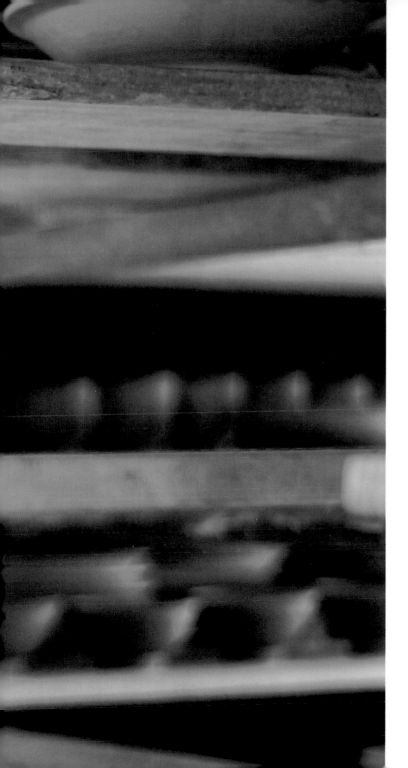

min *gei*

民 芸

the people;   art
the public

Koishiwara potters are not individually famous, but our pottery is known as one of the best examples of *mingei,* or "hand-crafted art of ordinary people."

小石原の陶工（焼物を作る人）は個人として知られていないかもしれませんが、小石原焼自体は有名な「民芸」の一つです。

Bernard Leach, the father of British studio pottery, once praised Koishiwara ware as "the perfection of Japanese beauty."

イギリスで「焼物の父」と呼ばれるバーナード・リーチ氏は小石原焼を日本の美そのものとして褒めたことがあります。

Mingei arts and crafts have these qualities:

- They are made by craftspeople who are not famous.
- They are produced in large quantities by hand.
- They are inexpensive.
- They are used in daily life.

Typical examples of Koishiwara ware include teacups, plates, bowls, sake holders, incense burners, large urns, and grinding bowls.

民芸品の特徴は

- 名が知られていない人が作るものです。
- 手作りで沢山の量が作られます。
- 安いです。
- 日常品として使われます。

小石原焼の代表的なもの中には、お茶碗、お皿、どんぶり、ちょうし、線香立て、大きなつぼ、すり鉢などがあります。

Pottery Basics
焼物の基本

We will introduce a few basic techniques
that are used to make stoneware.

陶器を作るための基本的な技法を
紹介します。

Raw clay is hard, so first the potter kneads it on the wheel.

生の粘土は堅いので、まずは、均等に柔らかくするために練っています。

Then he starts to shape it. In this photo, he is beginning to make a plate.

それから形を作り始めます。この写真はお皿を作り始めているところです。

After setting the basic shape, he uses a pallet to adjust it.

ある程度の形ができてから、へら（形成する道具）をあてて調節します。

Next, he uses a piece of deerskin called *nameshi* to straighten and smoothen the edge.

次に、「なめし」と呼ばれる鹿の皮で縁（ふち）を整えます。

45

Finally, he uses his hand to measure the size of the plate.

最後に、手で大きさを調整します。

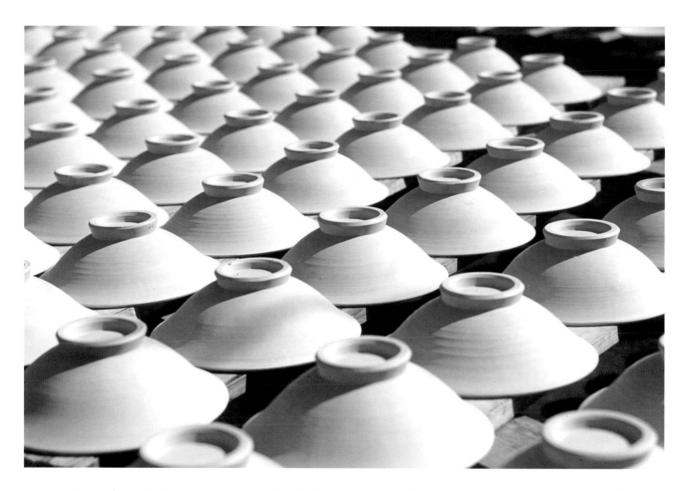

Even though they are handmade, if all the items of the same design are not exactly the same size and shape the potter cannot be called a true craftsman.

手作りだからといって、大きさや形が揃わなければ真の陶工とは言えません。

This is a traditional *noborigama*, or "climbing kiln." The heat from a fire at the bottom rises through each chamber, making it possible to fire many pieces at the same time.

これは伝統の「のぼり窯」です。下の方で燃やした熱がそれぞれの袋（部屋）に上っていくので、同時にたくさんの作品を焼くことができます。

This is the inside of one of the chambers. When the kiln is operating it gets up to nearly 1,230°C (2,246°F).

これは袋の中です。焼いているときには
1，230°C近くまで温度が上がります。

Most of Koishiwara's potters use the same techniques that were developed in this region in the seventeenth century.

ほとんどの小石原の陶工が、17世紀にこの地域で発明された技法をそのまま受け継いで使っています。

Our Own Style
私達のスタイル

One of Koishiwara's most famous techniques is called *tobikanna*. *Tobi* means "flying" and a *kanna* is a thin, springy, curved piece of metal. When the clay is partly dry, placing the kanna on it and rotating the wheel causes the kanna to skip across the clay's surface and create "chatter marks."

小石原でできた一つの有名な技法は飛び鉋（かんな）と言います。鉋は薄くて弾力性のある曲がった金属の道具です。粘土が生乾きの状態で鉋を軽くつけて轆轤（ろくろ）を回すと、鉋が飛ぶように表面を削って模様をつけます。

Here is the tobikanna pattern on an urn and a large plate.

飛び鉋模様がこの大きな壺と皿に見られます。

This plate shows another technique called *hakeme*. A *hake* is a flat paintbrush.

この皿で「刷毛目」という技法が見られます。

This pattern is made by slowly rotating the plate on the wheel and lowering a brush dipped in glaze onto it with a steady rhythm.

これはゆっくり轆轤を回して、一定のリズムで刷毛を上下に動かし、化粧土に濃淡を付けます。

This plate shows the *warabake* technique. *Wara* means "straw." This pattern is made by lowering a straw brush onto the spinning piece while the glaze is still wet.

このお皿には「藁刷毛」という技法が見られます。この模様をつけるために、化粧土が乾く前に藁で作った刷毛を上からのせて模様を付けます。

The patterns on these bowls were applied by the potter's finger. This is called a "finger-wipe" design.

これらのどんぶりの模様は陶工の指で描かれます。「指描き」といいます。

This potter is making a *suribachi,* or grinding bowl – one of Koishiwara's specialty products. A suribachi has many small grooves on the inside. Using it with a wooden pestle, you can grind seeds, nuts, and the like into a fine powder.

この陶工は小石原の特産品のすり鉢を作っています。すり鉢の内側には溝が沢山ついています。木製のすりこぎと一緒に使うと木の実や種を粉末状にすり潰すことができます。

These pots are usually placed on portable gas burners and used for cooking soups and stews right at the table with other people.

これらの鍋は通常ガスコンロと一緒にテーブルの上に置かれて、何人かの人達と共に料理しながら食べるために使われます。

These are individually handmade chopstick rests.

一つ一つ手作りされた箸置きです。

These are speaker cabinets made with the tobikanna pattern. High-frequency notes sound especially good through them.

伝統と現代風を上手く融合させた飛び鉋の模様がついているスピーカーです。特に高音がきれいに再生されます。

This is the *genkan,* where we take off
our shoes before entering the main
part of a house. These floor tiles are
made with the hakeme design. They
are beautiful and also functional because they don't slip.

これは玄関で、家に入る前に靴を
脱ぐ場所です。これらのタイルは
刷毛目デザインで作られました。
美しく、また滑らない機能も持ち
合わせています。

About 150 of the 2,600 people living in Koishiwara are potters, and fourteen of them are recognized as Master Craftsmen by the Japanese government.

小石原の２、６００ほどの人口のうち、約１５０人が陶工です。そして14名が政府から栄誉ある工芸家として認められています。

小石原焼

雨窯　太田富隆作
飴釉掛け流し大壷

69

This is a large store that was built to display and sell pottery produced all over the village. It's a nice place to enjoy the rich variety of Koishiwara ware, and it's popular among tourists.

ここは、村のあちこちで作られる焼物を一同に展示して直接売るために作られた大きなお店です。バラエティー豊かな小石原焼を楽しめる素敵な場所で、観光客に人気があります。

Unfortunately, some of the potters who had been selling their works there have had to close their kilns because of poor business, or because they have had to retire and don't have children who would take their places.

しかし、ここで作品を売っている陶工の中には、商売の問題や退職する年に
なっても代わりに引き継ぐ子供がいないため辞めてしまう人がいます。

Cedars, Storms, Statues
杉・台風・木像

Several centuries ago, one of Koishi-wara's forests was used as the gateway to Mt. Hiko, a sacred site for the practice of *shugendō* (an ancient Japanese religion).

数世紀前に小石原の森は、修験道で神聖な英彦山という山の入り口として使われていました。

Photo by 唐山健志郎　http://ja.wikipedia.org/wiki/修験道

shu
修
"training"

gen
験
"enlightenment"

dō
道
"the path"; "the way"

Shu-gen-dō means "the path to enlightenment through training."

People who practice shugendo take long retreats in the mountains to undergo various types of hard training – such as sitting or standing under cold waterfalls and fasting. They do this to more deeply understand the relationship between humans and nature, and to gain spiritual powers.

修験道という言葉は「訓練をすることによって悟りを得るための方法」という意味です。

行者は長い期間山の中にこもり、冷たい滝に打たれたり断食など様々な厳しい修行をします。それにより人間と自然の関係をもっと深く理解し、霊的な力を付けることが目的です。

From 200 to 600 years ago, shugendo priests on their way to Mt. Hiko planted cedar trees in this Koishiwara forest as evidence of their spiritual training.

２００〜６００年前に、英彦山に向かっている行者達は修行の証として、この小石原の森に杉を植えていました。

The tallest of the remaining trees stands over fifty-five meters (180 feet) and has a circumference of eight meters (26 feet).

現在残っている一番高い杉は高さ５５ｍで周囲８ｍです。

Koishiwara

In 1991, a powerful typhoon with 240 km/h (150 mph)
winds blew straight through Koishiwara and destroyed
more than 200 of the 600 giant cedars.

１９９１年に２４０km/hの台風が小石原を直撃し、６００本
あった行者杉のうちの２００本が倒されました。

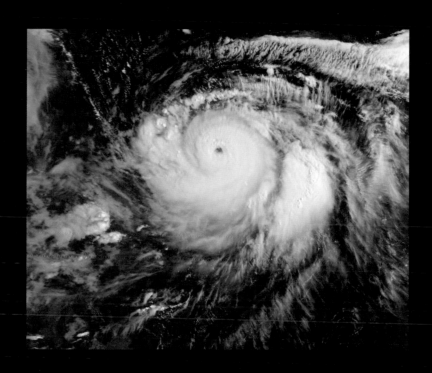

Typhoon Mireille, 1991

These statues are standing in front of
"Moriyama Meiboku," a wood craft
shop in Koishiwara. Moriyama is the
name of the family that owns the shop,
and *meiboku* means "precious wood."

The statues were made from giant trees
blown over in typhoons. They have
been carved into symbols of good luck
in Japanese folklore and mythology.

これらの木像は「森山銘木」という木
工製品の店の前に飾ってあります。森
山はお店のオーナーで、銘木は貴重な
木という意味です。

木像は、台風で倒れた大きな木から作
られました。日本の神話や民話での幸
運のシンボルとして彫られました。

This is Daikoku, the god of good fortune and guardian of farmers. He is usually shown standing on bales of rice, carrying a sack of treasure slung over his shoulder, and holding a magic mallet. It is said that, when struck, the mallet can produce anything desired.

これは大黒様で、富をもたらす農家の守り神です。たいてい俵の上に立っていて、肩の上に財宝が入っている布袋をかけ、打出の小槌を持っています。小槌をたたくと願ったものが出てくると伝えられています。

This is Ebisu, the god of fishing and commerce and brother of Daikoku. Ebisu is always bearded and smiling, and usually dressed as a peasant holding a fishing rod and a large, red sea bream. He is a symbol of safe sailing, good fishing, and success in business.

これは恵比寿様と言って漁業と商業の神様で、大黒様の兄弟です。いつも髭を伸ばしていて笑顔で、農民の格好をして釣り竿と鯛を持っています。恵比寿様は安全かつ大漁と事業の成功を祈願するシンボルです。

These are *maneki neko*. *Maneki* means "beckoning" and *neko* means "cat." Maneki neko always have one of their paws raised and bent as though they are calling someone over.

To people who live in other countries it may seem as if maneki neko are waving goodbye; this is because of a difference in culture. In Japan, people can call each other over by holding up their hands and bending their wrists down and up – just like these maneki neko.

招き猫は、いつも人を呼び寄せるように、どちらかの手を挙げています。

外国に住んでいる人にとって、逆に「さようなら」を表しているように見えるかもしれません。これは文化の違いです。日本では、人を呼ぶ時にこのように手を挙げて、手首を下げたり挙げたりします。

It is said that maneki neko with their left paws raised beckon customers, and ones with their right paws raised beckon good fortune.

左手を挙げている猫はお客さんを招いて、右手を挙げている猫は金運を招くと言われています。

School Closing
学校閉鎖

This is Koishiwara Elementary School. It was established in 1903, but it will close in 2011 because there are not enough children to keep it running.

This is the school that all of the children in Koishiwara and generations of their ancestors have attended, and so its closing is a very sad thing for everyone in the village.

これは小石原小学校です。

１９０３年に設立されましたが、子供の人数不足のために２０１１年に閉鎖してしまいます。

小石原の子供達、そして何世代もの先祖達が通っていた学校ですので、村の皆にとって、とても悲しいことです。

This is the main entrance. Photos of all the graduating classes since the school was established are displayed along the wall, and Koishiwara ware is exhibited at the top of the stairs.

校舎の表玄関です。 壁には学校が設立されてから今までの卒業生の写真が飾ってあり、階段の上には小石原焼が展示してあります。

明治３６年３月

This is the first graduating class. The caption reads "Meiji 36th year third month." "Meiji 36th year" means the 36th year of Emperor Meiji's reign (1903 in the Western calendar). The "third month" (March) is the end of the Japanese school year.

第一期卒業生です。表題には、「明治３６年３月」と書いてあります。「明治３６年」は明治天皇が天皇になってから３６年目という意味です。「３月」は日本の学年度の終りです。

Graduation photos document the conclusion of our lives as elementary school students, and so they are very precious to us.

These are the 2010 graduating students and their teachers.

卒業写真は私達が小学生として一緒に送ってきた学校生活の区切りを記録
するものなので、とても貴重な写真です。

こちらは２０１０年の卒業生と先生達です。

As the number of children has decreased year by year, the desks have spread out more and more.

Most Japanese school desks are made of wood and metal, but these desks, chairs, and floors are all made from the trees in Koishiwara's forests.

この学校の生徒達が年々少なくなると同時に、机が段々離れてきてしまいました。

ほとんどの日本の学校の机が木と金属で作られますが、これらの机、椅子、床などが完全に小石原の森の木から作られました。

The sign in the lower right photo says, "first year classroom."

94

Of course, pottery is one of our favorite classes. Students can make whatever shapes and styles they like.

もちろん、陶芸の授業が一番好きな授業の一つです。子どもの思いがそのまま形となって焼物になっていきます。

These are a few creations made by third-graders.

３年生の生徒達が作った作品です。

"Sacred Gemstone Mountain"
宝・珠・山

In the year 547, a large meteorite landed right on top of a mountain overlooking a region that is now part of Toho Village. The villagers who lived nearby believed it had magical powers and built a shrine into the side of it. They also named their village *Hō-shu-yama,* or "sacred gemstone mountain."

西暦５４７年に、現在の東峰村のある地域に大きないん石が、山の頂上に落ちました。近くの住民達は、その石に不思議な力があると信じて、その麓に神社を作りました。そして、自分達が住んでいる村を「宝珠山」と名付けました。

This is the shrine's *torii,* or entrance gate. All Shinto shrines have a torii standing at the entrance to their grounds.

After walking up a hill from the torii for about five minutes…

その神社の鳥居です。全ての神社の入り口には鳥居があります。

鳥居から5分ぐらい上り坂を歩くと…

...you arrive at this spot.

From here you go up those stairs –
which have been cut into the rock of
the mountain – to reach the shrine.
It's better to stretch your legs before
coming here!

…この場所に着きます。

ここから階段（岩を削って作った）
を登って行けば神社につきます。
ここに来る前に足をストレッチし
ておいた方がいいですよ！

Along the way up the stairs, you can see hundreds of small statues of ancient guardian deities perched on the slope.

階段を登っている途中の坂の斜面には数百の小さいお地蔵様が見られます。

Once you pass here...

ここを通り過ぎると…

...at last, you reach the shrine.

…ようやく、神社につきます。

You must be tired; but it was worth the climb, wasn't it?

疲れたでしょうけど、登って来て良かったでしょう？

Our Own Food
特産の食べ物

Hoshuyama's main claim to fame is its terraced rice fields. These fields have been selected among "Japan's 100 Best Rice Fields" by the Ministry of Agriculture and Fisheries. This region's clean air and water, and also the high altitude, make an ideal environment for growing delicious rice.

These are the rice fields in early May, when the sprigs have just been planted.

宝珠山の一番の有名なものは棚田です。これらの棚田は農林水産省より「日本の棚田百選」の中に選ばれました。この地域のきれいな空気と水、そして標高は美味しいお米を育てる理想的な環境です。

これは、5月の始めに稲が植えられたばかりの棚田です。

Here is a closer view of the newly planted sprigs. The rice fields are irrigated throughout the growing season.

植えられたばかりの稲をもっと近くで見た様子です。稲の成長の期間中、水をはります。

These are the rice fields in mid-August.

８月半ばの棚田です。

This is how the fully-grown rice plants look around late September, when they are ready to be harvested.

９月末頃に、稲刈りできる状態に十分成長した稲は、こんな感じです。

After the plants are cut, they are hung out to dry in the sun.

稲刈りをした後、太陽の下で乾燥させます。

Then the rice is hulled and prepared for sale.

This farmer is delivering rice and vegetables to a local market.

それから外皮を取って、販売出来る状態にします。

この人は、穫れたお米と野菜を、村のお店に届けている農家の人です。

棚 *means "terrace."*
田 *means "rice field."*
米 *means "rice."*

Almost all of the food in Toho's markets is locally produced. Much of it is brought in and stocked on the shelves by the farmers themselves.

東峰村のお店で売られている食べ物のほとんどは、現地で作られているものです。その大部分は農家の人が直接持って来て棚に並べます。

This farmer is explaining to a young mother how to transplant vegetable seedlings.

農家の人が若いお母さんに野菜の苗の移し替え方を教えているところです。

These are pickled *rakkyō,* a vegetable that looks like a small onion. Rakkyō are tasty with (Japanese-style) curry rice, grilled fish or meat.

ラッキョウという、タマネギと形が似ている野菜を漬け物にしたものです。ラッキョウはカレー・焼き魚・肉などと一緒に食べると美味しいです。

Here is one of the Toho Village's specialties, *yamakake soba*. (*Soba* is a kind of noodle made from buckwheat.) The broth is made from local chicken stock and has a slightly sweet flavor that brings out the taste of the soba noodles. It is topped with grated Japanese mountain yam, chopped green onions, and small Japanese mushrooms called *nameko*.

東峰村のみんなが大好きな山かけそばです。スープのダシは地鶏で取っているので、少し甘めで、そばの味を引き立てます。上には、すった山芋と刻んだネギとなめこをのせます。

In the 1950s, while digging a train tunnel through a mountain in Hoshuyama, a mineral spring was discovered. The water is really delicious and was included in the Ministry of the Environment's "100 Best Spring Waters of the Heisei Era." It is especially good in coffee and Japanese-style cooking.

１９５０年代に、宝珠山の山の中で鉄道トンネルの掘削中に水が湧き出ました。その水はとても美味しく、環境省の「平成の名水１００選」に選ばれています。 コーヒーや和食に特に合います。

The water is always flowing
from these spigots, and it is
available for anyone to come
and fill their containers.

湧き水はこれらの蛇口から
常に流れ出ていて、誰でも
利用できます。

The people, pottery, and foods of Toho Village all get together in harmony at mealtimes.

食事のときに、東峰村の人と焼物と食べ物は一体となります。

Extended Family
大家族

In our village, all the kids are like cousins and their parents are like aunts and uncles. Although crime in Japan as a whole is increasing, there is no sign of that trend here. People leave their doors unlocked, kids often have meals or stay over at each other's houses, and our parents team up to take us on excursions, go swimming, prepare for festivals, and so on.

村の全ての子供は従兄弟のようで、彼らの両親は叔父叔母のような関係です。日本全国では犯罪が増えていますが、ここではその傾向がありません。村の人達は家の鍵をしめないし、子供達はよくお互いの家で食事したり泊まったりするし、両親達が協力し合って遠足や水泳やお祭りを企画してくれます。

Setting out to go swimming in a river...

川に泳ぎに行く出発直前と…

...and coming back.

…戻ってきたところです。

Chatting with a friend on the phone.

友達と電話でお喋りしています。

Chilling out with a dog in the shade.

日陰で犬と遊んでいます。

Hanging out with our families. "It's hot today, isn't it!"

家族とくつろいでいます。「今日は暑いね。」

Those buckets contain different colors of glaze.

バケツの中には焼物にかける化粧土が入っています。

Playing in a stream on the side of the road. There are many different kinds of small fish here, such as the "weather loach" (a fish used in some Japanese dishes).

道路沿いの小川で遊んでいます。ドジョウなどの色んな小さな魚がいっぱいいます。

Exploring in rice fields is also fun. Various birds and, during the growing season, frogs and even tiny fish can be found here.

田んぼを探索することも楽しいです。いろんな鳥、そして稲の成長期には
カエルや小さな魚などを見つけることができます。

And of course, eating meals together. In our village, people almost never eat alone.

そして、もちろん、みんなで一緒にごはんを食べます。私達の村では、
一人で食べることは、ほとんどありません。

jinbei
甚平

yukata
浴衣

Summer Festival
夏祭り

The mid-August summer festival is a long awaited event for everyone in our village.

Some people like to dress up in *jinbei* or *yukata* (two types of light cotton kimono). The fabric feels good on the skin, and when we wave the *uchiwa* it feels like a fresh breeze is blowing.

８月中旬の夏祭りは、村の皆にとって待ちに待った行事です。

甚平か浴衣に着替えて向かう人もいます。生地は肌触りが良くて、うちわを扇ぐ時、さわやかな風に包まれているような気がします。

It's late afternoon, and people are starting to gather.

夕方で、人が集まり始めています。

"I wonder if that guy has shown up yet...?"

「気になる子は、まだ来てないかな…？」

Peace!

ピース！

Members of the festival staff making *yakisoba* (pan-fried buckwheat noodles).

焼きそばを作っているお祭りの実行委員です 。

Kids competing in a shaved ice (like a snow-cone)-eating contest.

子供達が「かき氷」の早食い競争をしているところです。

Children prepare hard for several weeks to perform on *taiko* drums at the summer festival.

子供達は、夏祭りで太鼓を叩くために数週間、一生懸命練習してきます。

Just before the performance . . .

まもなく本番です…

Performing in front of everyone can be nerve-wracking, but it's an unforgettable experience.

皆の前で演奏してドキドキするけど、忘れられない経験です。

These drums are irreplaceable treasures that have been played by generations of our elders. As we perform, the way they once felt when they did resonates within us.

この太鼓は、先輩達が叩いてきたかけがえのない太鼓です。叩いている間、先輩達がどんな思いで叩いてきたか、私達にはよく伝わってきます。

Capturing the moment. She'll be up there in a few years...

この瞬間を記録しています。彼女も、数年後そこにあがっているでしょう…

Many young people have to leave the village when they grow older, to attend university or work in the city. But for kids and families, we think this is a great place to live.

多くの若者は、大学に行くためや都会で働くために村を出て行かなければなりません。しかし、ここは子供や家族にとって最高な環境だと思っています。

We have many worries, but we love Toho Village.

And so, we believe, we'll all surely return someday.

心配なことは色々ありますが、
東峰村が大好きです。

だから…いつかはきっと皆
戻ってくると信じています。

Word Search

うちわ	*uchiwa*	Japanese fan
げんかん	*genkan*	place to take off shoes before entering a house
すりばち	*suribachi*	grinding bowl
たいこ	*taiko*	Japanese drum
とうほうむら	*tōhōmura*	Toho Village
とりい	*torii*	shrine entrance gate
そば	*soba*	buckwheat noodles
にほん	*nihon*	Japan
ゆかた	*yukata*	summer kimono
まねきねこ	*manekineko*	"beckoning cat"

く	な	れ	に	と	り	い	と
う	え	あ	ほ	ざ	つ	ひ	う
ち	げ	ま	ん	た	ぺ	ぬ	ほ
わ	や	ん	ね	て	い	を	う
る	す	の	か	き	せ	こ	む
も	し	り	ぷ	ん	ね	め	ら
は	ぞ	ろ	ば	さ	そ	こ	だ
じ	ゆ	か	た	ち	ば	か	よ

Crossword

ACROSS

1   "beckoning cat"

5   "treasure gemstone mountain"

6   grinding bowl

7   the god of fishing and commerce

8   pan-fried buckwheat noodles

11   the god of good fortune and guardian of farmers

13   the name of our village

14   a large city near our village

15   the name of the current era in Japan

16   a noodle made from buckwheat

DOWN

2   _____ ware

3   "art of the people"

4   the Japanese emperor who lived from 1852–1912

6   "the path to enlightenment through training"

9   shrine entrance gate

10   where you take off your shoes in a house

12   Japanese fan

13   Japanese drum

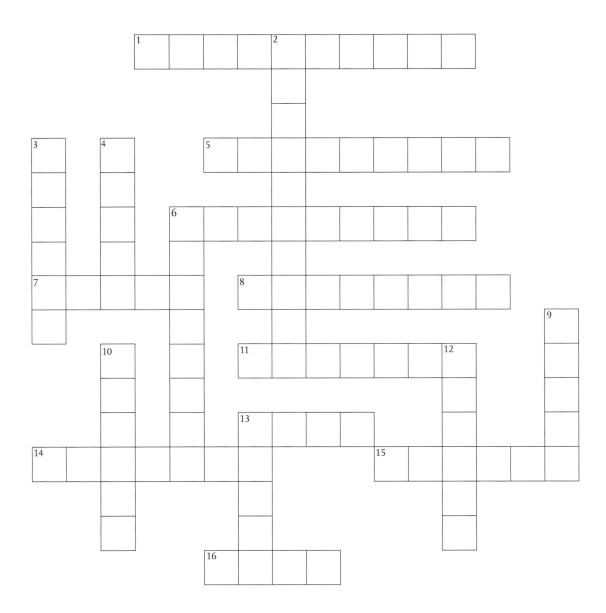

Match them up!

Try to match these words to their Japanese equivalents.

1. Japan __ a. 民芸

2. America __ b. 夏祭り

3. Hoshuyama __ c. 焼物

4. Koishiwara __ d. 棚田

5. Toho Village __ e. 修験道

6. Fukuoka __ f. 小学校

7. pottery __ g. 小石原

8. mingei __ h. 東峰村

9. shugendo __ i. 宝珠山

10. terraced rice fields __ j. 日本

11. elementary school __ k. 福岡

12. summer festival __ l. アメリカ

Test

1. What is the population of Japan (2010)?

   (a) 67,000,000

   (b) 127,000,000

   (c) 347,000,000

2. How much of Japan is covered by mountains?

   (a) 1/2

   (b) 2/3

   (c) 3/4

3. Which of these is NOT a major cause of depopulation in small Japanese communities?

   (a) falling birthrate

   (b) high taxes

   (c) limited job opportunities

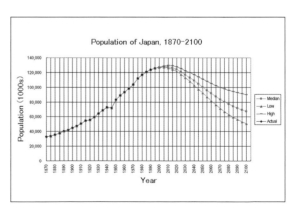

4. When did Hoshuyama and Koishiwara merge?

    (a)   1979

    (b)   1992

    (c)   2005

5. Where in Japan is Toho Village located?

    (a)

    (b)

    (c)

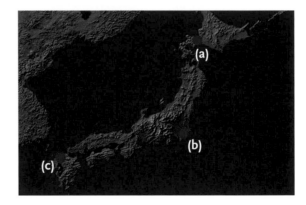

6. What was the population of Toho Village when it was established?

    (a)   2,749

    (b)   6,749

    (c)   10,749

7. How long does it take to get to Fukuoka using this train?

   (a)   25 minutes

   (b)   1 hour

   (c)   2 hours

8. In which century was Koishiwara ware first made?

   (a)   17th century

   (b)   18th century

   (c)   19th century

9. What does *mingei* mean?

   (a)   traditional stoneware

   (b)   art of the people

   (c)   the perfection of Japanese beauty

10. About how hot does this kiln get when it is firing pottery?

    (a) 800°C (1,472°F)

    (b) 1,000°C (1,832°F)

    (c) 1,200°C (2,192°F)

11. What is this pattern called?

    (a) *tobikanna*

    (b) *hakeme*

    (c) *warabake*

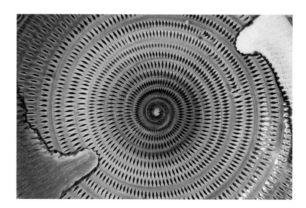

12. What is this bowl used for?

    (a) grinding tea leaves into a powder

    (b) grinding nuts, seeds, and the like

    (c) whipping tea with a bamboo whisk

13. About how many giant cedars still stand in Koishiwara's forests?

    (a) 200

    (b) 400

    (c) 600

14. What does this gesture mean?

    (a) "hello"

    (b) "come here"

    (c) "goodbye"

15. What year is Meiji 36 in the Western calendar?

    (a) 1903

    (b) 1916

    (c) 1936

16. About how many years ago did this meteorite fall from space?

    (a)   300 years ago

    (b)   750 years ago

    (c)   1,500 years ago

17. What does *hō-shu-yama* mean?

    (a)   sacred cedar forest

    (b)   pristine water mountain

    (c)   sacred gemstone mountain

hō shu yama
宝珠山

18. Which of the following means "terraced rice field rice"?

    (a)   修験道

    (b)   棚田米

    (c)   小石原

19. Around when is rice harvested in Toho Village?

    (a)   late May

    (b)   mid-August

    (c)   late September

20. What is the girl in the pink yukata holding?

    (a)   *jinbei*

    (b)   *uchiwa*

    (c)   *yukata*

21. What is this man making?

    (a)   *rakkyo*

    (b)   *yakisoba*

    (c)   *yamakake soba*

Word Search

く	な	れ	に	と	り	い	と
う	え	あ	ほ	ざ	つ	ひ	う
ち	げ	ま	ん	た	ぺ	ぬ	ほ
わ	や	ん	ね	て	い	を	う
る	す	の	か	き	せ	こ	む
も	し	り	ぷ	ん	ね	め	ら
は	ぞ	ろ	ば	さ	そ	こ	だ
じ	ゆ	か	た	ち	ば	か	よ

Crossword

ACROSS

1   MANEKINEKO
5   HOSHUYAMA
6   SURIBACHI
7   EBISU
8   YAKISOBA
11 DAITOKU
13 TOHO
14 FUKUOKA
15 HEISEI
16 SOBA

DOWN

2   KOISHIWARA
3   MINGEI
4   MEIJI
6   SHUGENDO
9   TORII
10 GENKAN
12 UCHIWA
13 TAIKO

Match them up!

1.	Japan	m	日本
2.	America	l	アメリカ
3.	Hoshuyama	i	宝珠山
4.	Koishiwara	g	小石原
5.	Toho Village	h	東峰村
6.	Fukuoka	k	福岡
7.	pottery	c	焼物
8.	mingei	a	民芸
9.	shugendō	e	修験道
10.	terraced rice fields	d	棚田
11.	elementary school	f	小学校
12.	summer festival	b	夏祭り
13.	yukata	j	浴衣

Test

1.	b
2.	c
3.	b
4.	c
5.	c
6.	a
7.	c
8.	a
9.	b
10.	c
11.	a
12.	b
13.	b
14.	b
15.	a
16.	c
17.	c
18.	b
19.	c
20.	b
21.	b

Acknowledgments

Children

Many children in Toho Village contributed to this book; these children constituted the core production team.

ITŌ, Masaya 伊藤正也

KAJIWARA, Manami 梶原まなみ

KAJIWARA, Yume 梶原優芽

MORIYAMA, Airi 森山愛理

MORIYAMA, Yūki 森山結希

MOTONAGA, Nagahiro 元永成洸

ŌTA, Yoshiya 太田義八

TESHIMA, Yui 手嶋ゆい

TESHIMA, Shūta 手嶋秀太

Photography workshop, August 2009

Post production (using Adobe Lightroom and Adobe Photoshop CS4)

Robert Schuman ロバート・シューマン

Media workshop, August 2007

KOYAMA, Keiko 小山敬子

MATSUO, Reina 松尾玲奈

MINO, Yasuhiro 三野泰宏

NAKAI, Hiroto 中井裕人

TANAKA, Satomi 田中里実

YOSHITOMI, Ryo 吉富諒

Copyediting

Kathleen Cushman カスリーン・クッシュマン

PLAISTER, Fumiko プライスター芙美子

SEGAWA, Tamaki 瀬川環

TAGAMI, Akiko 田上晶子

Design assistance

Sandra Delany サンディー・デレイニー

Logistical and editorial assistance

FURUKAWA, Nami 古川奈実

IWASHITA, Akihiro 岩下玲礼

KOBAYASHI, Junichi 小林純一

KAJIWARA Narumi 梶原成美

KOGA, Yukari 古賀由佳里

MATSUMOTO, Mayumi 松本真由美

ONO, Toyonori 小野豊徳

Laura Rog and her students at Albion Elementary School, Albion, New York
ローラ・ロジュとニューヨーク州のアルビオン市のアルビオン小学校の生徒達

Potters

KAJIWARA, Hizuru	梶原日出
OTA, Kazutaka	太田和孝
OTA, Taketoshi	太田剛速
OTA, Tomitaka	太田富隆

Farmers

HAYAKAWA, Hisaki	早川久喜
HAYAKAWA, Mieko	早川美恵子

Special thanks to the staff of the Toho Village Government Office for their enduring support and cooperation.

Useful Resources

Toho Village official website (in Japanese)
http://www1.vill.toho.fukuoka.jp/

Videos taken during 2007 media workshop
http://toho.org

What Kids Can Do
http://wkcd.org

In Our Village
http://www.inourvillage.org

Asia Society
http://asiasociety.org/education-learning/students

Asia Kids Society
http://kids.asiasociety.org

ABCJP.net
(a youth media–based introduction to Japanese culture through the hiragana alphabet)

See you.

じゃ、ね。